Original title:
Wonders of Elsewhere

Copyright © 2024 Creative Arts Management OÜ
All rights reserved.

Author: Ethan Prescott
ISBN HARDBACK: 978-9916-90-536-4
ISBN PAPERBACK: 978-9916-90-537-1

Embracing the Invisible Threads

In quiet whispers, love does bloom,
A tapestry woven through the room.
Threads of kindness, soft and bright,
Binding souls in the gentle light.

Moments shared, a fleeting glance,
Connections made in a tender dance.
Invisible ties, so strong yet fine,
Weaving our hearts, a sacred sign.

Through laughter's echo, through sorrow's sigh,
These threads endure, they never die.
Intertwined paths, so close and far,
Guiding us gently, like a shining star.

Embrace the bonds that we cannot see,
In each heartbeat, in each plea.
For in these threads, our stories blend,
Forever cherished, they will not end.

Intrigues Over the Distant Land

Whispers travel through the night,
Secrets held in moonlit flight.
Shadows dance on ancient stone,
Mysteries of lands unknown.

Footsteps trace where few have gone,
Echoes fade with early dawn.
Chasing dreams of distant shores,
Adventure waits behind closed doors.

The Alluring Reminiscence

Faded memories softly glow,
Moments captured long ago.
Laughter lingers in the air,
Whispers of a time we share.

Old photos tell a tale so bright,
Colors warm in morning light.
Every glance, a fleeting day,
Echoed love will find its way.

Elysium of the Unexplored

Beyond the hills, a world awaits,
Where nature sings and time abates.
Rivers flow like silver threads,
Woven dreams in soft green beds.

Mountains rise with rugged grace,
Hidden paths embrace the space.
Here, the wild and free unite,
In a dance of pure delight.

Rhapsody from Untamed Edges

Whirlwinds swirl through fields of gold,
Stories whispered, brave and bold.
Nature's voice, a song untold,
Echoes linger, fierce and cold.

Waves crash down with thunderous might,
Stars ignite the velvet night.
In the wild, we find our truth,
A rhapsody of lost youth.

Echoes of the Untraveled

Whispers dance on winds of time,
Footprints fade where shadows climb,
Paths unworn, a silent plea,
Wander far, but never free.

Lost in dreams, the heart takes flight,
Chasing stars through endless night,
Each step forward, past the gate,
Echoes call, but never wait.

Balconies Overlooking Infinity

Perched above the vast unknown,
The sky a canvas, dreams are sown,
Clouds as sails, my spirit roams,
In this place, my heart finds homes.

Gaze upon horizons wide,
Where secrets of the cosmos bide,
Moments linger, time stands still,
Balconies of thought fulfill.

Secrets of the Silent Voyager

Deep within the ocean's sigh,
A ship unseen, it drifts on high,
Waves, they speak in muted tones,
Casting tales of ancient bones.

In the depths, the mysteries hide,
Silent hearts, they seek the tide,
Footsteps light on hidden sands,
Curiosity expands.

Horizons that Call Aloud

Sunrise breaks the edge of night,
Dawn unfolds, a golden light,
Across the land, the promise grows,
Horizon calls, where adventure flows.

Mountains high and valleys low,
Echoes whisper, winds will blow,
Every step, a story true,
Horizons vast invite the view.

Shadows Across Unseen Lands

Shadows creep where none can see,
Ancient whispers float like leaves.
Hidden paths beneath the trees,
Seeking secrets time conceives.

Moonlight dances on the ground,
Echoes of a world unknown.
Footsteps soft, without a sound,
Guiding hearts that roam alone.

Dreams of Fabled Places

In twilight's glow, the visions stir,
Fragments of a world so bright.
Adventures call, the heart will purr,
Exploring wonders through the night.

Mountains high and rivers wide,
Embers of a sleeping flame.
In the depths where dreams abide,
Every soul can find their name.

Light through a Forgotten Veil

A gentle breeze begins to swell,
Softly lifting shades of gray.
Through the mist, a story tells,
Of brighter paths that linger, play.

Sunbeams pierce the morning hush,
Colors burst, the world awakes.
In the quiet, there's a rush,
Reality, a world that shakes.

The Quiet Call of the Untraveled

Through silent woods where echoes hide,
The untraveled path lies still.
Drawn by whispers deep inside,
A thirst for more, an ancient thrill.

Each step forward brings the chance,
To touch the dreams that softly sway.
As shadows blend in twilight's dance,
The heart will find its own sweet way.

The Mapless Explorer's Heart

In the wild, where shadows play,
A spirit roams, both night and day.
No compass guides, just instincts true,
Adventures wait in every hue.

Winds whisper secrets, trees sway slow,
With every step, new paths to sow.
Unearthed tales in the rustling leaves,
A journey unfolds, where wonder weaves.

Stars above in a dance so bold,
Illuminate dreams, yet untold.
With every heartbeat, a story starts,
In the mapless land, lives the explorer's heart.

Chronicles of the Unfamiliar

In the quiet corners of the night,
Whispers linger, shadows take flight.
Footsteps echo on cobbled streets,
In strange lands, where mystery greets.

Every alley, a tale to spin,
With faces glowing, where dreams begin.
Eyes of travelers, stories unfold,
Chronicles captured, both brave and bold.

From distant shores, the lessons learned,
In the flames of hope, our spirits burned.
Through the echoes of time we stare,
Finding solace in the unfamiliar air.

Sketches from the Other Side

In twilight's glow, sketches appear,
Images fleeting, whispering near.
A canvas of dreams, softly glows,
With colors of worlds, nobody knows.

Brush strokes of longing, tempered sighs,
Framed by the echoes of haunting cries.
Unseen borders, where realms collide,
Every picture tells of hearts that abide.

Voices travel through colors and light,
Tales of the lost, sailing through night.
Every sketch carries a piece of the soul,
From the other side, they make us whole.

Lighthouses Beyond the Mist

Amidst the fog, they stand so tall,
Beacons of hope, guiding us all.
Through tempest highs and tranquil seas,
Their light cuts through like a gentle breeze.

Stories etched in the ocean's spray,
Guardians of dreams that drift away.
With every flash, a promise made,
That love endures, never to fade.

Secrets of sailors, lost and found,
In lighthouses where memories abound.
They stand as reminders, steadfast and bright,
Through storms of life, they shine their light.

Echoes of the Unexpected Journey

In shadows of the winding road,
Whispers of the past unfold.
Each step taken, tales revived,
Moments lost, where dreams survived.

With every twist, a chance to see,
Paths diverge, wild and free.
The heart beats with eager grace,
In hidden truths, we find our place.

Soft echoes guide us through the night,
Stars above, a hopeful light.
From distant shores, we sail anew,
The journey speaks, always true.

From every stumble, lessons learned,
In quiet corners, passion burned.
Together we embrace the fight,
For every ending brings new sight.

Mirages of Infinite Possibilities

Across the sands of shifting time,
Wonders rise like whispered rhymes.
Each illusion, a chance to see,
A canvas brushed with dreams set free.

In every choice, a world awakes,
Through paths untraveled, fate remakes.
The mind explores horizons vast,
In fleeting moments, futures cast.

Glimmers dance on distant shores,
Each heartbeat opens hidden doors.
The beauty lies in what could be,
In fragile hopes, we find the key.

Let visions guide us to the night,
Where every dream holds cast a light.
In endless skies, our spirits soar,
Through mirages, we seek for more.

The Spirit of Places Unseen

In shadows deep where secrets sleep,
A spirit stirs, a promise keeps.
Beyond the veil of sight and sound,
In every place, a truth is found.

The rustling leaves and ancient stones,
Whisper stories of distant bones.
Echoes beckon from yesteryears,
In every sigh, the world appears.

From mountains high to oceans wide,
Nature calls with arms open wide.
Through every turn, the heart can sense,
The quiet strength of existence.

In unseen realms, our spirits dance,
Through hidden paths, we take our chance.
For every place holds tales untold,
In searching hearts, the magic unfolds.

Murmurs Beneath the Global Skies

Beneath the moon, the world awakes,
A symphony of whispered fakes.
From cities bright to quiet lands,
Connection flows through unseen hands.

In every sigh, a story shared,
Voices rise, and hearts are bared.
Across the globe, dreams intertwine,
In every pulse, a life divine.

The winds carry tales from afar,
Guided by the light of stars.
The universe sings a timeless song,
In every moment, we belong.

Through night and day, the dance goes on,
In murmurings, we find our dawn.
Together we soar, hand in hand,
Across the skies, united we stand.

Glimmers Beyond the Known

In shadows cast by fading light,
Dreams ignite with sparks so bright.
Whispers float on evening's breath,
Chasing hopes that conquer death.

Stars awaken in the night,
Guiding hearts with gentle light.
Each flicker holds a story old,
Of secrets waiting to be told.

Beyond horizons, visions sway,
Unraveled truths like threads of clay.
In silence, beauty finds its voice,
Inviting souls to make a choice.

Glimmers shine where fears do fade,
In the dance of light and shade.
Step forth, embrace the unknown trail,
In every moment, let your heart sail.

A Journey Through the Forgotten Sky

Through clouds of time, we drift and roam,
In search of where our spirits comb.
Winds carry tales of ages past,
A tapestry of dreams amassed.

Beneath the stars, old wishes gleam,
In whispered notes of a distant dream.
Every heartbeat echoes lost desires,
Kindled by the moon's soft fires.

Horizons await to be revealed,
Where secrets lie, our fates concealed.
The constellations weave their song,
In the night sky, where we belong.

With every breath, we carve our path,
In unity with the universe's math.
A journey forth through shadows shy,
Crafting stories in the forgotten sky.

The Enigma of Uncharted Paths

Whispers echo in the forest's heart,
Drawing wanderers who seek to start.
Uncharted paths lay wide and deep,
Awakening dreams that dare to leap.

Footsteps blend with nature's rhyme,
Mysteries beckon in their prime.
Every corner holds a realm unknown,
In spirit's light, we feel at home.

A riddle wrapped in emerald leaves,
In silence, nature's truth believes.
Follow the call of the unseen way,
Where shadows dance and spirits sway.

Embrace the enigma, let it unfold,
New beginnings born from tales of old.
In every turn, a story's grasp,
The uncharted path is ours to clasp.

Colors of Another Dawn

In hues of pink and gold we rise,
The dawn awakens painted skies.
Brushstrokes of a world anew,
In every shade, a dream comes true.

Light drapes softly over the earth,
A canvas woven since our birth.
Each day unfolds a vibrant song,
In colors bright, we all belong.

Whispers of light ignite the day,
As shadows melt and fears give way.
In every moment, beauty found,
A symphony of life unbound.

So breathe in deep the morning's grace,
With open hearts, we embrace this space.
For every dawn brings fresh delight,
In colors splashed across our sight.

Heritage of the Untrodden Path

In shadows where the grasses sway,
A whisper dances in the fray.
With every step, the stories breathe,
Of spirits lost, and dreams we weave.

Beneath the ancient, knowing trees,
The echoes thread the gentle breeze.
Each stone and leaf, a tale to tell,
Inheritances that bind us well.

The road is rough, yet beauty thrives,
Where silence sings and stillness drives.
With open hearts, we navigate,
This path of past, we celebrate.

And as we walk, the roots unfold,
Each step a link to stories old.
Together bound, we find our way,
Inherit this dance, day by day.

Ethereal Light of Distant Realities

Beyond the veil where shadows play,
A flicker glows, a beckoning ray.
It whispers secrets, softly spun,
Of worlds unseen, where dreams are won.

In twilight's grace, the stars align,
A tapestry of fate divine.
Through cosmic realms, our spirits soar,
In endless wonder, we explore.

The light cascades in hues so bright,
Illuminating paths of night.
With open minds, we dare to seek,
The truths that live, both mild and bleak.

In realms of thought, where visions shine,
We grasp the threads, the intertwine.
Ethereal light guides every quest,
Awakening the soul's behest.

The Sound of Distant Drums

I hear the pulse of heartbeats far,
A rhythm echoing, like a star.
In twilight's hush, they call to me,
The sound of drums, wild and free.

Each thump a promise, fierce and bold,
Stories of courage, waiting to be told.
In lands unknown, they weave their spell,
A siren's rhythm, ringing well.

Through mountain peaks and river bends,
The distant drums, their music mends.
They bind us close, though miles apart,
In unity, they speak to heart.

With every beat, I'm drawn anew,
To dance with shadows, to chase the view.
The sound of drums, a timeless score,
Awakens dreams forevermore.

A Palette of Unfamiliar Colors

In dusk they blend, these colors rare,
A vivid stroke beyond compare.
With every hue, anew they show,
The tales that only artists know.

Emerald whispers, crimson sighs,
Each shade a story that never dies.
On canvas wide, imagination soars,
A palette rich with hidden shores.

Blues of depths where oceans dream,
Yellows that burst like morning's beam.
With every brush, a universe born,
A symphony painted at the dawn.

These unfamiliar shades confess,
The beauty found in each caress.
In vibrant chaos, we discover light,
A dance of colors, pure delight.

The Manifest of Mystic Journeys

In realms where shadows dance and sway,
Whispers of wisdom lead the way,
Each step a tale, a thread of light,
To chase the dawn, embrace the night.

Stars awaken in the silent dream,
Rivers flow with a silver gleam,
Carrying secrets of ages past,
On wings of time, our souls are cast.

Through veils of mist, we travel far,
Guided by an ancient star,
Each heart a compass, every breath,
Unlocking truths of life and death.

When paths converge in twilight's glow,
Mysteries of the universe unfold,
In journeys mystic, new worlds begin,
The sacred dance, the loss, the win.

Enchanted Intersections of Life

At crossroads where the spirits meet,
Life's vibrant stories feel complete,
Threads of fate intertwine and weave,
In moments cherished, we believe.

Beneath the arch of starlit skies,
The laughter echoes, and love flies,
Every soul a spark, a glowing fire,
In shared connections, we rise higher.

Nature whispers in the breeze so sweet,
Tempting hearts where shadows greet,
In every glance, a tale unfolds,
Enchanted stories yet untold.

As seasons shift and clocks will chime,
A dance of lives, a song of time,
In every intersection, dreams collide,
In the embrace of life, we abide.

Serenades from Beyond the Ordinary

Soft melodies drift through the night,
Notes of magic take their flight,
In every pause, a moment to feel,
The heart beats loudly, raw and real.

Voices whisper in the twilight dim,
Chanting secrets where lights grow grim,
A symphony of thoughts entwined,
Echoes of love that gently bind.

Through shadows deep, the music calls,
Resonating in forsaken halls,
Each harmony a step we take,
Awake the dreams that never break.

From realms unseen, the chords arise,
Awakening wonder in disguise,
In every serenade, a spark ignites,
Beyond the ordinary, life invites.

The Enchantment of Hidden Dimensions

In corners where the silence breathes,
Whispers of magic weave like leaves,
Each layer holds a novel sight,
Dimensions dance in hidden light.

Fragments echo through the ethereal mist,
Promise of realms not to be missed,
Explorers dream in crystalline hues,
In every shadow, a world renews.

The tapestry of time weaves tight,
Patterns shifting, day and night,
In hidden depths, the treasures gleam,
An endless journey, a fragile dream.

Through portals open, eyes can see,
The infinite dance of reality,
In enchantment's fold, we find our way,
To hidden dimensions, come what may.

Stories Untold in the Shadow of Giants

In whispers soft, the legends call,
Beneath the trees where shadows fall.
They dance in light, they weave and spin,
The tales of old, where dreams begin.

A giant's footstep, a tremor wide,
Echoes of laughter, a flowing tide.
Each story blooms, like moss on stone,
In quiet corners, the seeds are sown.

Forgotten voices in rustling leaves,
Woven in time, the heart believes.
Mysteries wrapped in historical clay,
Awake in the twilight, they pave the way.

From distant worlds, the past implores,
Unlocking paths to hidden doors.
In silent nights, the stories unfold,
In the shadow of giants, where dreams are told.

Canvases of Enigma and Light

Strokes of color, bold and bright,
Whispers of the day and night.
Images dance, in void they play,
A canvas breathes in soft array.

Lines converge with tales untold,
Mysteries wrapped in hues of gold.
Each corner hides a view anew,
The heart ignites, the vision grew.

In layers deep, the stories blend,
Brushes touch, as colors mend.
Fleeting moments, captured tight,
In canvases of enigma and light.

With every stroke, the soul takes flight,
In splashes of joy, in dark of night.
Art unfolds its vibrant wings,
Through silence, the spirit sings.

Bridges to the Mystic Unknown

Stretching high, the arches gleam,
Connecting worlds, like a silken seam.
Steps lead forth to lands unseen,
Through misty veils, where shadows lean.

Voices call from distant shores,
With secrets locked behind closed doors.
Mystic whispers, soft and low,
Guiding hearts where few would go.

Beneath the stars, in twilight's glow,
Every bridge a chance to grow.
Paths entwined, in fate's design,
Bridges to the unknown divine.

In every step, the brave explore,
Finding truths forevermore.
In the heart's quest, where spirits roam,
We discover there is always home.

Canvas of Serendipitous Encounters

A fleeting glance, a smile's spark,
In crowded streets, where dreams embark.
Uncharted paths that cross by chance,
The universe weaves in happenstance.

Through serendipity, we find our way,
In random moments, the heart will sway.
Each meeting penned in cosmic ink,
A canvas filled with life's sweet link.

Laughter shared on sunlit days,
Unexpected joy in curious ways.
In every soul, a story weaves,
Serendipity's embrace believes.

Together we dance, in vibrant hues,
Creating memories, a woven muse.
In every heartbeat, love takes flight,
A canvas painted with pure delight.

Secret Gardens in Far-off Lands

In the hush of emerald leaves,
Whispers dance in gentle breeze.
Petals fall like quiet dreams,
Where sunlight glows and laughter beams.

Hidden paths of fragrant blooms,
Carry secrets, brush away glooms.
A symphony of colors bright,
In gardens far, out of sight.

Beneath the arch of ancient trees,
Life awakens, spirits tease.
With every step, a story told,
In these realms, both warm and bold.

So let us wander, hand in hand,
To secret gardens, wonderland.
Where time stands still and hearts ignite,
In far-off lands, pure delight.

Journeys to Enigmatic Isles

Sailing through the misty haze,
Chasing shadows, wandering ways.
Isles emerge from ocean's sigh,
Where dreams are spun and spirits fly.

Tides whisper tales of ages past,
Of treasures lost and found at last.
Palm trees sway in rhythms old,
Secrets wrapped in tales retold.

Footprints trace the sandy shore,
A call to venture, evermore.
Through coral reefs and hidden caves,
In these isles, adventure saves.

So join me on this winding quest,
To enigmatic isles, no rest.
With hearts as sails and stars as guides,
We'll navigate the ocean's tides.

Mysteries Beneath Celestial Skies

Beneath the blanket of the night,
Stars awaken, shining bright.
Galaxies spin in silent grace,
Unraveling time and space.

Moonlit whispers, secrets shared,
Celestial wonders, none compared.
Constellations weave their tales,
In cosmic winds, our spirit sails.

Planets dance in endless waltz,
Echoing truth in grand results.
Curiosities call us near,
To puzzle pieces drawn so clear.

So look above with wonder wide,
For mysteries in stars abide.
In the night, our dreams take flight,
Beneath celestial skies so bright.

Starlit Paths to the Unknown

Winding trails beneath the stars,
Lead us near, beyond our scars.
Each twinkle whispers, soft and low,
Of places we have yet to go.

Footsteps echo on the way,
Guided by the light of day.
In shadows deep, adventure calls,
As starlit dreams embrace our thralls.

Through the veil of night we stride,
With hope and courage as our guide.
The unknown beckons, thrilling chase,
In starlit paths, we find our place.

So let us tread where few have been,
To lands unseen and tales within.
Our hearts will lead, our spirits soar,
On starlit paths, forevermore.

Glistening Sands of the Sacred Coast

Glistening sands under the sun,
Waves whisper tales, one by one.
Seagulls dance in the warm breeze,
Nature's song brings hearts to ease.

Shells scattered, memories kept,
Footprints linger where we slept.
The tide returns to kiss the shore,
Cradling secrets, evermore.

Beneath the sky, so vast and wide,
Dreams awaken with the tide.
Sunset paints the sea with gold,
Stories of love forever told.

In the twilight, silence reigns,
Softly echoing the rains.
A journey ends, yet carries on,
In the heart, the coast lives strong.

Footprints in the Fabric of Time

Footprints etched in grains of sand,
Mark the tales of where we stand.
Each step taken, a story spun,
Under the watch of the setting sun.

Moments linger, shadows cast,
Whispers of the years gone past.
Threads of life woven so tight,
Binding day and embracing night.

In the tapestry of our dreams,
Life unfolds in vibrant themes.
With every heartbeat, time aligns,
Weaving love in life's designs.

As stars emerge in evening's glow,
Footprints fade, yet we still know.
Time moves on, yet we remain,
Forever linked, in joy and pain.

Echoes of Distant Shores

Echoes drift from distant shores,
Carried deep by ocean's roars.
Songs of sailors lost at sea,
Whispered tales of destiny.

The horizon gleams with dreams untold,
Each wave a secret, brave and bold.
A compass forged in starlit skies,
Guides the heart where freedom lies.

Winds of change sweep through the night,
Holding hope in their soft flight.
From afar, the beauty calls,
As the nightingale softly falls.

In the stillness, echoes blend,
Past and future softly mend.
Together, we drift on time's tide,
Towards the shores where dreams abide.

Whispers from the Horizon

Whispers rise from the horizon's edge,
Carrying secrets we often pledge.
A soft glow in the morning light,
Promising dreams that take flight.

Clouds drift lazily, tales untold,
Sketching shadows in hues of gold.
A navigator of hope's embrace,
Guiding hearts to a sacred place.

With each dawn, the world anew,
Whispers coax the soul to pursue.
Nature sings in vibrant hues,
Inviting us to chase the muse.

As twilight descends, whispers fade,
Memories linger where joy was made.
In dreams, we find the strength to soar,
Chasing whispers forevermore.

Breaths from Forgotten Realities

In shadows where the whispers weave,
Fragments of what we dare believe.
Time flows like water, silent yet clear,
Each sigh a story, held so near.

Ancient echoes in the night,
Guiding us towards the light.
Through the mist of faded dreams,
We find the truth in silent screams.

A dance of stars in twilight's glow,
Revealing paths we long to know.
As memories drift like autumn leaves,
In breaths of air, the heart believes.

In the absence of all time,
The rhythm of the cosmos chimes.
Through forgotten realms, we softly tread,
On whispers where the spirits led.

Pathways of Surreal Discoveries

Wandering down a twisting road,
Reality bends, a heavy load.
Dreamscapes bloom in colors bright,
Hopes wander far into the night.

Mirrors reflect a world undone,
Two suns rise as shadows run.
Thoughts unspool like threads of gold,
In hidden tales long left untold.

Each step reveals a brand new scheme,
Crafting visions from the dream.
Voices echo through the maze,
In soft murmurs, lost in gaze.

Through the forest of the mind,
Wonders wait for those who find.
With every turn, a treasure springs,
Pathways woven with ancient wings.

The Call of Ancient Echoes

Across the hills where silence reigns,
Ancient whispers break the chains.
Stories woven in the breeze,
Calling forth the hearts that seize.

Forgotten realms of time and space,
Hold the echoes of a face.
Each star a guide, each moon a friend,
To the stories that never end.

In shadows deep, reflections glide,
The call of ages cannot hide.
Time stands still in the glowing dark,
Illuminating every spark.

Listen close to the echoes' song,
In their cadence, we belong.
The past and present intertwine,
In ancient echoes, truth shall shine.

Dreams Beyond the Vast Expanse

Beneath the stars where shadows play,
Dreams awaken, drift away.
Across the sky, the wishes sail,
In infinite realms where we unveil.

Horizons stretch like a longing sigh,
Embers of hope that never die.
Through galaxies of thoughts untamed,\nWe seek the wonders, unashamed.

In the silence, visions bloom,
Guided by a soft, sweet tune.
Each heartbeat thrums like a distant drum,
In the vastness, we become.

The essence of life breaks free,
Whispers of what's yet to be.
Beyond the expanse, we take flight,
In dreams that dance with endless light.

Tides of Time in Ancient Waters

The ocean whispers secrets low,
In waves that dance with tales of old,
Each tide a memory, ebb and flow,
In depths where timeless stories unfold.

Echoes of ships that sailed the night,
With dreams woven in salt and foam,
Beneath the surface, history's light,
Still guides those lost, eternally home.

Ancient shores reflect the sky,
Where lovers carved their names in stone,
As moonbeams paint the night's sweet sigh,
In whispers of time, they are not alone.

Let currents guide the heart's desire,
Through seas of memory, deep and wide,
In every wave, a flickering fire,
The past and present, intertwined.

Fragments of Lost Civilizations

Ruins stand as shadows tall,
Where once proud laughter filled the air,
Stone by stone, the stories call,
Of lives once lived with fervent care.

Fragments of art, painted bright,
Tell of a people's dreams and fears,
In silence, they still seek the light,
Through dust and time, they've shed their tears.

In overgrown paths, history sighs,
As roots reclaim the stones of pride,
Once vibrant hearts now lost to skies,
Yet their essence will not subside.

Listen closely to the earth,
For every stone has tales to impart,
In crumbled halls, we find rebirth,
Remnants of love, a beating heart.

Ephemeral Beauty of the Unseen

In twilight's grasp, shadows blend,
Where colors bloom, yet quickly fade,
The fleeting moments that we tend,
Like softest whispers, serenely swayed.

A butterfly flits through the glade,
With wings like dreams that drift away,
In each soft flutter, time does fade,
Yet in that flight, the heart will stay.

Stars wane as dawn begins to tease,
With gentle rays that kiss the night,
Each fleeting breath within the breeze,
Holds beauty cloaked in soft twilight.

So cherish now the calm and still,
For moments pass like whispers spun,
In unseen worlds, the heart can thrill,
To dance in light, 'til day is done.

The Allure of Unmapped Territories

Beyond the hills, where wild winds sing,
Lies land untouched by maps and dreams,
In whispered tales, adventure's ring,
Awaits the bold with daring schemes.

Forests deep with emerald shade,
Hold mysteries in every glen,
From mountain peaks to rivers laid,
The heart seeks all that's free from pen.

In valleys rich, where shadows play,
And stars unveil their cosmic dance,
The call of nature leads the way,
Inviting souls to take a chance.

So wander on, let spirit roam,
In lands where few have dared to tread,
For every step can lead you home,
To dreams of paths yet to be spread.

Portals to the Unfathomed

In twilight's glow, the gates appear,
Whispers call from realms so clear.
A gateway spun of silver thread,
Where silence rests, and dreams are fed.

Through shadows cast in muted light,
Adventurers find their hearts ignite.
Each step a journey, lost yet found,
A cosmic dance, unbound, profound.

Within the mist, the echoes churn,
For every heart there lies a turn.
Embrace the void, the endless sea,
For life is vast, and so are we.

The portals spin, in endless grace,
Inviting all to seek their place.
In the unfathomed, we take flight,
Beyond the realms of day and night.

Footprints in a Forgotten Dream

Along the shore where tides once kissed,
Footprints linger in a gentle mist.
Memories woven in the sand,
A tale of love, a fragile band.

Each wave that breaks erodes the past,
Yet echoes of the heart will last.
In shadows deep, we wander still,
Seeking solace, chasing will.

Through valleys where the silence sings,
Lost in the whispers of fleeting things.
The dream decays, but hope remains,
In forgotten paths, the spirit gains.

With every step on this sacred ground,
A promise made, a promise found.
Though time may fade the marks we leave,
Our hearts retain what we believe.

Promises from the Other Side

Beyond the veil where visions weave,
Lies a world that we perceive.
Promises echo, soft and sweet,
In the quiet, our hearts meet.

Beneath the stars, the vows are cast,
Threads of fate are woven fast.
A gentle breeze, a sighing breath,
Brings warmth and love, defying death.

In twilight's grasp, the spirits blend,
What once was lost begins to mend.
In dreams, we touch the hands of fate,
With every promise, we create.

Let shadows dance and spirits glide,
For truth awaits on the other side.
In whispered tones, our hopes align,
In endless realms, our souls refine.

Secrets of the Wayfaring Soul

In winding paths where shadows play,
The wayfaring soul finds their way.
Secrets buried, tender and deep,
In quiet moments, we choose to keep.

With every step, a story unfolds,
Of dreams long chased and tales retold.
The road is vast, yet so confined,
To wander here is to seek the mind.

Through echoes of laughter, through tears of woe,
The soul gathers wisdom, silently grows.
With every journey, a piece is found,
In the silence, the heart unbound.

For every traveler on fate's embrace,
There lies a truth in time and space.
The secrets shared, both near and far,
Will guide us home, like a shining star.

Enchanted Forests of the Void

Whispers dance on ancient trees,
Veils of twilight, secrets tease.
Shadows stretch in moonlit glades,
Where time entwines in mystic shades.

Flickers of light in ghostly hue,
Footsteps echo, depths imbue.
Echoes linger, tales unfold,
In forests dark, their magic bold.

Silence wraps the heart in peace,
As all the world's loud noises cease.
In this realm, lost souls reside,
With unseen guides as paths collide.

Nature's pulse, a gentle sigh,
Beneath the vast and starlit sky.
In the void, they find their song,
Where all the weary wanderers belong.

Skylines of a Distant Tomorrow

Underneath the brightening sun,
City dreams have just begun.
Steel and glass that scrape the sky,
Fleeting hopes as moments fly.

Echoes from the neon heart,
Promise futures set apart.
Tracks of light on busy streets,
Every heartbeat, rhythm beats.

In the haze of twilight's glow,
Visions form as breezes flow.
Stories written on the breeze,
In every glance, a wish to seize.

Horizons shift in silence deep,
While hum of bustling life won't sleep.
Together holding dreams in hand,
Skylines rise, an endless land.

Serendipity in Strange Places

Footsteps stray on paths unknown,
In hidden nooks where fate has grown.
Chance encounters spark the light,
In the quiet, love ignites.

Rustling leaves and laughter shared,
Moments simple, hearts laid bare.
In alleys framed by whispered tales,
Life unfolds where serendipity prevails.

Colors blend in twilight's art,
Connections formed, a brand new start.
From the mundane, beauty thrives,
In strange places, magic dives.

With every smile and fleeting glance,
We find ourselves in serendipitous dance.
Embrace the odd, the unplanned space,
For life reveals, in strange places.

Reflections on Foreign Winds

Winds that carry stories far,
Whispers of each wandering star.
Through valleys deep and mountains high,
In every breath, the world does sigh.

Voices merge from lands unknown,
In shared dreams, we're never alone.
Each gust a window to the soul,
Uniting hearts to make us whole.

Shifting sands beneath our feet,
Echoing life in moments sweet.
Gestures bridge the wide expanse,
When foreign winds invite romance.

Embrace the breath of distant shores,
In foreign winds, the spirit soars.
Reflections dance and time does bend,
As we let the wind transcend.

Cartography of the Soul's Desires

Maps unfold on silent nights,
Tracing paths of heart's delight.
Each curve a whisper, soft and true,
Guiding dreams towards the blue.

In shadows dance the hidden wishes,
Beneath the stars, the magic swishes.
A compass set to find the light,
Drawing journeys in the night.

The valleys hold the laughter's sound,
Sacred echoes joyfully found.
Mountains bear the burdens, deep,
While rivers sing the secrets they keep.

In every corner, stories lie,
Written in the open sky.
A cartographer of fate's embrace,
Each longing etched in time and space.

The Call of the Unseen Voyage

Whispers beckon from afar,
On the winds, a guiding star.
Unseen realms await the brave,
To surf the tides and ride the wave.

Footsteps dance on hidden shores,
Opening up forgotten doors.
Waters deep with tales untold,
Adventure's heart, fiercely bold.

Each dawn reveals a chance to roam,
Through tempests fierce, we'll find our home.
The horizon speaks in language rare,
It's in the journey that we dare.

With sails unfurled, we chase the breeze,
In every challenge, find our ease.
The horizon glimmers, vast and wide,
In the call of the unseen, we glide.

Gemstones of Forgotten Horizons

Hidden gems beneath the sands,
Await the touch of gentle hands.
In silence, old stories gleam,
Woven deep in each lost dream.

Crystals whisper from the stone,
Echoes of the lives they've known.
Timeless secrets, brightly shine,
In the deep, where legends entwine.

Skies of twilight hold their key,
Unlocking realms of memory.
The past and present intertwine,
In the glow of history's line.

Underneath the vast expanse,
Each gemstone holds a silent dance.
Forgotten horizons call us near,
To cherish all the dreams held dear.

The Pulse of Infinity's Borders

Time stretches like a tender thread,
Binding moments, joy and dread.
Across the vastness, whispers flow,
In the silence, we come to know.

The pulse of life beats strong and clear,
In every heartbeat, love draws near.
Beyond the edges, fate will weave,
An eternal dance, we believe.

Dimensions blend in twilight's glow,
As stars align in cosmic show.
The infinite calls with a soft embrace,
Within its arms, we find our place.

Borders fade in the light of day,
As dreams transcend and drift away.
In every pulse, the universe sings,
Embracing hope and all it brings.

Beyond the Veil of Familiarity

In shadows cast by the setting sun,
We wander paths where dreams have spun.
The air is thick with whispered lore,
Beyond the veil, we seek for more.

In every glance, a story hides,
A truth concealed, where time abides.
We touch the edges of the night,
In search of stars, in search of light.

Through tangled woods, with weary feet,
We chase reflections, bittersweet.
In distant echoes, we find our call,
As shadows dance upon the wall.

Beneath the moon's soft, silver grace,
We step into another place.
With open hearts and dreams set free,
Beyond the veil, we long to be.

Secrets in the Winds of Change

The gusts of fate, they twist and turn,
With every breath, a lesson learned.
In every fold, a secret hides,
The winds of change, where hope abides.

They carry whispers from afar,
Echoing tales of who we are.
With every breeze, a path reveals,
Unraveled truths, our heart appeals.

Embrace the storm, let courage flame,
For in the chaos, none's to blame.
Each shift, a chance to redefine,
The power of choice, our fate entwine.

So dance with winds, let spirits soar,
Each secret breeze opens a door.
With faith in change, we'll bravely sing,
In the arms of new beginnings.

Songs of the Wayward Trails

Through winding paths where shadows creep,
The songs of trails awaken sleep.
Each step we take, a story's told,
In notes of laughter, dreams behold.

The echoes call from mountains high,
In valleys deep, where spirits lie.
We chase the sun, we chase the night,
With open hearts, our souls take flight.

In scattered leaves, a melody flows,
As nature hums what no one knows.
With every turn, a new refrain,
In songs of life, we find the gain.

So wander forth, let voices blend,
On wayward trails, the journey's end.
In harmony, our hearts will play,
The songs of life shall light the way.

The Allure of Hidden Realms

In twilight's hush, where secrets sigh,
Hidden realms beckon from the sky.
With every heartbeat, we draw near,
To places where the unknown steers.

Veils of mist curl through the trees,
Carrying whispers on the breeze.
In shadows deep, the spirits dwell,
In every heart, there's magic's spell.

With open minds and eager eyes,
We'll chase the dreams that never die.
Each hidden realm, a tale unspun,
In enchanted worlds, our souls are one.

So wander forth, let wonder reign,
Embrace the allure, break every chain.
For in these realms, so rich, so rare,
We find the dreams that linger there.

The Lure of the Unfamiliar

A whisper calls from distant shores,
With secrets wrapped in twilight's lore.
Paths untrodden, shadows weave,
Adventure's breath, we dare believe.

Each step a dance with hidden fears,
In silence thick, the heart it steers.
The unknown sings, a siren's tune,
Under the watchful gaze of the moon.

New visions spark in twilight's glow,
Awaking dreams we do not know.
The thrill resides in what is strange,
The lure of change, the wild exchange.

So come, dear heart, let courage rise,
In uncharted realms, we find our prize.
Together we'll weave a tale anew,
In the realm of the unknown, just me and you.

Tales from the Edge of Time

Ticking clocks and whispers low,
Where past and future twist and flow.
Secrets linger, shadows play,
In timeless realms where we can sway.

Echoes of worlds that never were,
In every heartbeat, soft and sure.
Moments captured, lost in dreams,
The thread of fate unravels seams.

From dawn till dusk, we chase the light,
Through golden glades and starry night.
Each memory a fleeting wisp,
A gentle pull, a tender lisp.

So gather 'round, these tales we spin,
Of love and loss and where we've been.
At the edge of time, we find our way,
In stories whispered, come what may.

Marvels Beyond the Ordinary

In every leaf and every stone,
A hidden spark of life has grown.
Each corner turned, a wonder found,
In simple things, magic is bound.

The dance of shadows, sunlit grace,
Every smile, a warm embrace.
In laughter shared, the world ignites,
A tapestry of pure delights.

Through tiny cracks, wildflowers bloom,
Defying all that spells out doom.
In mundane things, a glimmer shines,
A universe in whispered signs.

So pause a bit, let wonders in,
In ordinary, the extraordinary spins.
With open hearts, we learn, we see,
The marvels of this tapestry.

Embraces from Beyond the Stars

When night unfolds her velvet sea,
The stars reach out, inviting me.
In cosmic dance, their light cascades,
A touch from realms where love pervades.

Galaxies spin in tangled threads,
Whispers of dreams where hope now tread.
The universe hums a soothing song,
In every heartbeat, we belong.

In lunar glow, our fears unwind,
Celestial arms, so sweet and kind.
Together we soar on stardust trails,
In every sigh, the cosmos sails.

So lift your gaze to heavens wide,
In every twinkle, let love reside.
With embraces from beyond the stars,
We find our home, no matter how far.

Dances across Celestial Waters

Beneath the moon's soft gaze, they sway,
Rippling dreams in silken spray.
Stars whisper secrets in the night,
While waves reflect the silver light.

In harmony, their forms entwine,
Ghostly figures, pure and divine.
Echoes of laughter fills the air,
As twilight weaves its gentle snare.

With every twirl, the currents spin,
Cradled by the night's cool skin.
A waltz of souls, both lost and free,
In celestial waters, wild and free.

As dawn approaches, shadows fade,
Yet in their hearts, the dance won't trade.
Though twilight ebbs, they leave a trace,
Of timeless love, in that ethereal space.

Pulse of the Untamed Land

Through sprawling fields where wild things grow,
The heartbeat of the earth does show.
Mountains rise with ancient pride,
As rivers carve the world, a guide.

Beneath the stars, the creatures roam,
In every corner, finding home.
The rustling leaves sing wild and low,
A symphony of strength and flow.

Each morning light, a canvas bright,
Brushes the land in warmth and light.
Where whispers echo through the trees,
The pulse of life on gentle breeze.

And should you wander, hear the call,
Of nature's voices, big and small.
Feel the ground beneath your feet,
The untamed pulse, a rhythmic beat.

Fragments of Unseen Myths

In shadows deep where legends wake,
Whispers weave through misty lake.
Forgotten tales unfold like leaves,
In silence wrapped, the heart believes.

A flicker of light, a phantom glow,
Echoes of stories lost in flow.
Figures dance in twilight's veil,
Secrets hidden from the trail.

From ancient stones and time's embrace,
Mosaic fragments find their place.
Each grain of sand, a tale untold,
In silent currents, they unfold.

The wind carries whispers, soft and light,
Of lost adventures, day and night.
In every echo, a world reborn,
Fragments of truths, forever worn.

Luminescence in Uncommon Places

Amid the cracks and shadows bare,
Glimmers of light spark the air.
In forgotten streets, they softly glow,
Secrets hidden, waiting to show.

Beneath the surface, life shall bloom,
In every crevice, dispelling gloom.
Tiny sparks in the darkest night,
Guide wandering souls with their light.

Vines cascade on stone and brick,
Life's resilience, vibrant and thick.
Among the ruins, colors blaze,
Transforming paths in wondrous ways.

Look closely now, don't turn away,
Even in gloom, hope finds a way.
In every heart, let kindness dwell,
For luminescence can break the shell.

Whispers from Uncharted Realms

In the silence of the dawn, soft secrets play,
Fleeting shadows dance where wild spirits sway,
Rustling leaves share tales of ages past,
In every breeze, a memory is cast.

Through the mist, a vision starts to bloom,
Echoes linger, weaving through the gloom,
Footprints trace the paths of dreams once bold,
In uncharted realms, adventure unfolds.

Stars align to guide the wandering heart,
Each whisper beckons, a call to depart,
Across the valleys, through the hidden glades,
Mysteries beckon, where time never fades.

With every step, the pulse of earth resounds,
In harmony, the unknown still astounds,
A journey begun, where few have dared roam,
In whispers of night, we find our true home.

Echoes of Forgotten Landscapes

Beneath the crumbling stone of yesteryears,
A tapestry woven with laughter and tears,
Silent valleys hold the songs of the past,
In echoes, the shadows of memories cast.

Moss-covered ruins tell stories untold,
In whispers of wind, the ages unfold,
Ancient trees watch over fields of gold,
A canvas of time where secrets are sold.

Glacial rivers carve through the heart of clay,
Tracing the paths where lost footsteps stray,
Each ripple carries a voice from the deep,
In forgotten landscapes, the phantoms we keep.

The horizon blushes at dusk's soft embrace,
As twilight unveils its enchanting grace,
In every echo, a reminder to roam,
In the heart of the land, forever our home.

Dreams Beyond the Horizon

On the edge where the sky meets the sea,
Dreams take flight, wild and free,
Waves carry whispers of hopes untold,
As the future awaits in glimmers of gold.

Chasing the sun as it dips into night,
Stars awaken to share their light,
In the still of the moment, visions expand,
Where imagination roams, we make our stand.

Footsteps on sand, with each new dawn,
Possibilities stretch from dusk to dawn,
With every heartbeat, new tales arise,
In the tapestry woven 'neath infinite skies.

Together we venture, hearts all aglow,
In pursuit of the dreams that ebb and flow,
Beyond the horizon where wishes ignite,
We'll find our way, guided by starlight.

The Hidden Treasures of Distant Shores

Beyond the waves, where the horizon lies,
Treasure awaits beneath infinite skies,
A glimmer of hope in a seashell's embrace,
Stories and wonders the tides soon erase.

Each grain of sand tells tales of the past,
Whispers of sailors whose shadows are cast,
Drifting on currents, their journeys unfold,
In search of the treasures that glimmer like gold.

Coves rich with secrets and dreams yet to find,
Connect the hearts that fate has entwined,
With every breath, the ocean calls clear,
To chase every treasure that wanders near.

In the embrace of the tides, we will roam,
A voyage of love, far away from home,
For distant shores hold the magic we seek,
In the treasures hidden, our spirits grow strong.

Cadence of Emerging Landscapes

Whispers of dawn caress the hills,
Nature's chorus gently spills.
Colors bloom, a tender rise,
As the world unveils its guise.

Rivers dance with playful grace,
Each bend a new, enchanting space.
Mountains whisper tales of old,
Secrets in the silence told.

Soft winds carry scents of pine,
With every breath, the earth divine.
Roots entwine in timeless songs,
In harmony where life belongs.

Sunset paints the sky with fire,
In every shadow, dreams aspire.
As the night begins to creep,
The landscape breathes, the world falls asleep.

Glances at Forgotten Horizons

Beyond the veil where memories fade,
Hidden paths in twilight laid.
Echoes linger, soft and low,
Footsteps trace where few may go.

Clouds drift by in a hush of grace,
Stories lost in time and space.
Glimmers spark the darkened skies,
Awakening the long-lost ties.

Fragments of light dance on the seas,
Whispers carried by the trees.
In the stillness, voices call,
Inviting dreams that rise and fall.

Shadows stretch across the land,
With open hearts, we understand.
To glimpse a world that once was bright,
Is to find solace in the night.

Beyond the Plains of Dusk

Fields of gold beneath the stars,
Silent echoes, ancient scars.
Each moment, a fleeting breeze,
Carrying whispers through the trees.

Crickets chirp as night takes hold,
Tales of beauty, softly told.
Moonlight bathes the world in white,
Guiding hearts through the velvet night.

Fading light, a tender kiss,
Painting dreams in realms of bliss.
Horizons stretch with hope anew,
Beyond the dusk, the vast, the true.

Restless souls in wander's chase,
Seeking warmth in nature's embrace.
Beyond the plains where shadows play,
Lies the dawn of another day.

Light and Shadow in Unknown Valleys

In valleys deep where shadows lie,
Golden beams of light draw nigh.
Misty mornings steal the breath,
Awakening life from silent death.

Echoes drift on gentle streams,
Life unfolds within our dreams.
Every turn, a dance of fate,
In the whispers of love await.

Beneath the boughs, the secrets dwell,
Of joy and sorrow, stories swell.
Painted skies in evening's glow,
Reveal the paths we long to know.

In every crevice, light will find,
The heart's desires intertwined.
As dawn reveals unknown terrain,
Light and shadow, joy and pain.

Fantasies Underneath Starlit Canopies

Beneath the glow of distant lights,
Dreams take flight in velvet nights,
Whispers soft in twilight's song,
The universe where we belong.

Waves of wonder, soft and clear,
Each twinkling star holds what we fear,
Yet in the darkness, hope ignites,
Guiding hearts through endless nights.

Silhouettes of trees sway slow,
Echoes of a world we know,
In every shadow, secrets spun,
As time and space become as one.

Together we weave stories bright,
In the comfort of starlit night,
Fantasies born on whispered breeze,
Beneath the canopies of trees.

The Dance of Otherworldly Memories

In twilight's embrace, we swirl and glide,
Echoes of ages where dreams reside,
Memories flicker, both near and far,
A dance of time beneath the stars.

With every turn and whispered sigh,
Phantom shadows in the sky,
We twirl with visions, long forgotten,
In realms of wonder, we are caught and...

Cascading dreams in colors bright,
We lose ourselves in cosmic light,
The essence of life in fleeting twirls,
Beneath the glow of otherworlds.

Moments captured in the air,
We dance with truth, we dance with care,
For in this realm where echoes swell,
Our lives unfold, a timeless spell.

Strokes of Adventure

With brush in hand, the world anew,
We paint our dreams in every hue,
Each stroke a journey yet untold,
Adventures waiting to unfold.

Mountains rise and rivers flow,
In lands untouched, our spirits grow,
Through forests deep and skies of blue,
Exploration calls for me and you.

We carve our names on cliffs of stone,
With every step, we find our own,
The map is drawn in heart and mind,
In strokes of courage, we unwind.

Together we chase the setting sun,
Finding magic, the dawn has begun,
With every turn, the world is wide,
In strokes of adventure, we confide.

Reflections from the Edge of Tomorrow

On the brink where futures meet,
We gaze ahead to paths so sweet,
Reflections dance in twilight's glow,
Whispers of dreams we do not know.

Time slips by with fleeting grace,
In every second, we find our place,
Beyond horizons, shadows play,
Guiding us to a brighter day.

In every heartbeat, choices swell,
Stories woven, yet to tell,
We rise and fall on winds of fate,
At the edge of tomorrow, we contemplate.

Hope springs forth in radiant light,
Illuminating the coming night,
Together we chase what's yet to be,
Reflections from time's deeper sea.

Reflections on the Other Side

In the mirror's gaze I see,
Fragments of what used to be,
Shadows dancing in the light,
Hints of dreams that took to flight.

Voices whisper through the glass,
Memories of moments past,
Time dissolves like morning dew,
Leaving traces, old and new.

Silent thoughts in tangled threads,
Replaying words that once were said,
Each reflection holds a key,
Unlocking paths that set me free.

On the edge, I stand and wait,
For the world to shatter fate,
With each pulse of time's embrace,
I find solace in the space.

Echoes in the Enchanted Forest

Through the trees, the whispers glide,
Mysteries that nature hides,
Footfalls soft on ancient ground,
Magic lingers, all around.

Branches sway with tales untold,
Secrets wrapped in leaves of gold,
Birdsong weaves a tranquil spell,
In the depths where wonders dwell.

Luminous glades invite the brave,
Where echoes of the past still wave,
Dancing shadows tell their lore,
Of those who ventured here before.

Underneath the silver moon,
Dreamers hum a timeless tune,
As the forest breathes the night,
In its heart, the world feels right.

The Allure of Lost Horizons

Beyond the hills where shadows play,
Lies a realm with skies of gray,
Where the sun is shy and slow,
Bathing earth in twilight's glow.

Wandering paths that seem to fade,
Silent calls that never trade,
Fleeting glimpses of the past,
Moments that are meant to last.

A gentle breeze spins tales anew,
Of dreams once sown in morning dew,
Hopes that rise with every dawn,
Yet linger on the edge, withdrawn.

Chasing visions, hearts aflame,
In the distance, I hear my name,
Each horizon, a siren's song,
Pulls me deeper, where I belong.

Interludes of the Unseen

Between the lines of day and night,
Moments tremble, out of sight,
In the hush, where whispers dwell,
Secrets weave a silent spell.

Veils of time, a fragile thread,
Stories shared by the unsaid,
Glimmers of what lies beyond,
In the depths, I feel so fond.

Echoes brush the edge of dreams,
Caught in nature's gentle streams,
Curtains drawn to hide the truth,
Wisdom rests in stolen youth.

Searching for what cannot be seen,
In shadows where the world's serene,
Each interlude a fleeting chance,
To feel the pulse of existence' dance.

Milton Keynes UK
Ingram Content Group UK Ltd.
UKHW022008131124
451149UK00013B/1058